/

Windows 10

Shortcuts

Learn impressive Windows 10 Shortcut Keys
in 60 minutes

Stephen W. Rock

Dedicated to all my readers

Acknowledgement

Ii want to say a very big thank you to Michael Lime, a 3D builder, my colleague. He gave me moral support throughout the process of writing this book.s

Table of Contents

INTRODUCTION

If you have the Windows 10 running on your computer and need some cool shortcut tips, then this guide is for you. Shortcuts are great. They help us achieve results faster. Apart from being productive, shortcuts help reduce the risk of Repetitive Strain Injury (RSI).

This book outlines, in an easy and straight-forward manner, the steps to be followed in executing any shortcut.

You're sure to learn impressive shortcuts in less than one hour. No complex rules. Just read and execute.

Enjoy the read!

Using shortcuts on the Windows 10 is a very fast way for you to increase your productivity when you work.

Here, well discuss the top Windows 10 shortcuts that will get you to switch between Windows, split the screens, do some multitasking in desktop and others.

When you want to learn the keyboard shortcuts, you could say it's like learning a new language. And just like learning a language, you don't get it all at first.

You'll start small as you build up your vocabulary. In time you'll get to understand and speak the language well.

So it is with the shortcuts for your Windows 10, you want to begin building your vocabulary with the things that you do regularly like switching from one program to another. When you do it'll stick to your memory and you'll remember.

Some of the things that you can learn first is minimizing Windows, looking for programs, multitasking through files, getting along with Windows search and finding some documents and files.

When you start to learn your short cuts with the things that you make use of regularly like these, you'll build your confidence with shortcut, speed up the activities that you carry out in Windows 10 and you'll get motivated to learn more since you're already seeing success with the small tasks.

Windows key + 1 or another number

Take a look at the taskbar, what you'll see is a row of applications and programs lined up. If you have an app that you make use of more than others, you can just add it to the row. In fact you could add it to the first place.

So let's say that **Google Chrome** is as the first app on your taskbar, you can just press **Windows key + 1** to get it open. You can also try this too with other apps. Like if an app is in the 3rd position, you can just use **Windows key + 3** to open it up.

If you would like to add your favourite app to the taskbar, follow these steps

1. Press the **Win** key and enter in the name of the app
2. Right-click the app

3. Choose the option for **Pin to taskbar**
4. The app will now be in the taskbar. You can also click and drag it to any position you want to on the taskbar

So you can add any program (except the File Explorer) to the taskbar and move it to any position you want. The reason you done want to add the File Explorer is because it already has its own shortcut. More on that in a bit

Windows key + left

There are variations to this command, you can also try **Windows key + right, Windows key + up** and **Windows key + down.**

What they all do is that they send the window or program that is currently open to the side of the screen. The left and right commands will send it to the left and right of the screen while the up and down commands will send the window reduce the size to the top and bottom of the screen.

If you have 2 apps open and you click **Windows key + left** or **Windows key + right** for a particular app, you'll be asked to set the other app to fill the empty area of the screen.

Windows key then type or Ctrl + E then type

The search option that exists in Windows is like the best thing ever. It definitely gets top rank in the list of useful. The reason for this is that you can basically find anything through it.

With this option, you don't have to fiddle around trying to find a particular file or app. You just use the search.

All you do is press the **Win key** and input the name of the program of app that you're looking for and tada!! It'll show up. It has no excuse not to.

In fact, you don't have to include the full name of the program before Windows brings it out to you. I'm looking for **Google Chrome** and all it did was type in '**Go**' and it supplies it at the top of the list.

Alt + F

This is a cool way to enter the file menu options in a program. Like for example in Microsoft word, where you have the **File, Home, Insert** and others. The **Alt + F** option will enable you to open the file menu.

It is kind of a stress to scroll all the way to the top just to reach the file option.

And it's not only the file you can reach with a shortcut.

When you press the **Alt** key, you'll see the key that you need to press to get the other options to show. Still in Microsoft word and you press the **Alt** key. It will you that **Alt + H** will enter the **Home** and **Alt + N** will open **Insert**.

Ctrl + Shift + Esc

This will get you to open the task manager quickly. You can also try to enter the search and type in '**Task Manager**'. But the **Ctrl + Shift + Esc** option is quicker.

Alt + Enter

When you select a file or a document and you want to see the properties, you don't have to right click and choose **Properties**. You can just easily press **Alt + Enter** and the properties window will open up.

It's in this properties segment that you'll be able to see the size of the file, the date when it was created, date it was modified and other properties of the file.

Another shortcut to summon the properties window is to use **Alt + right click**. It does the same thing; bring up the properties menu.

Windows key + E

When it comes to looking for apps and programs, the best place to turn to is the Windows search. But when it comes to looking files and documents, the File Explorer is great at it.

The reason for this is not only because the name says 'File' Explorer but also because it does some filtering features that allow users to be able to narrow down what they search for. This method is an efficient way to dig through and find files in your computer.

For you to summon the File Explorer in shortcut style, you just use **Windows key + E**. Now you'll see a wide array of options that you use to search for your file. You'll see navigational options, filers and views that you can use to improve your 'search experience'

In the search bar at the top right, you can input the name of a file you want to find. But something else that you can try to do again is to input the extension. Like you add the .jpg or .png if you are looking for a photo. Or, you can find a document with the .docx extension

Windows key + Ctrl + D

This button will help you to create another desktop. And by another desktop it's a virtual one.

Windows key + Ctrl + left or right

This will help to go scroll through the desktops. Pressing the left key will return to the previous desktops you were in.

Pressing the right key will scroll you through the newer desktops you just created.

Windows key + Ctrl + F4

So you're done with the virtual desktop, you want to close it, and you have no idea how. You just have to press **Windows key + Ctrl + F4** to quit it. Just make sure that you saved all you were doing on the new desktop.

Ctrl + E

Lovely way to turn on the search. You can make use of this option in the File Explorer. This will help you to search the current folder you are in.

When you hit the Ctrl + E option on your keyboard, the cursor will jump to the search box at the right hand corner of the screen. So you have a fast way to search for a file. Just press **Windows key + E** to enter File Explorer and **Ctrl + E** to search for the item.

This doesn't only work in File Explorer. It will also work when you are in a web browser (or at least for most modern browser). Try it for Microsoft Edge or Google Chrome. Pressing the **Ctrl + E** will send you to the address bar for you to enter the any URL.

Windows key + X

This option will get you to open up the start menu options. Normally you would have to right click the **Start** to show up this menu.

This is the menu that houses the mobility center, program and features, device manager, task manager and more.

Windows key + I

This is a quick way to launch the **Settings** window. If you are looking for a particular setting, you can use to the search to find it.

Alt + Tab

Another option that makes the list among the cool is the **Alt + Tab** function. What this does is it makes to be able to switch between Windows very quickly.

Let's say that you are working on Microsoft Word and Google Chrome. Normally, you'll have to go to the bottom of the taskbar to select the program you want to switch to or you can just minimize the current program you're in to get to the other one.

But with the **Alt + Tab** option you can switch easily. You can press the combo once and then you'll go to the other program that's opened.

You can also press it again to switch back to the previous window. That's for 2 programs. What happens when there are 3 or more programs opened?

Easy enough. When there are multiple programs opened, pressing the **Alt + E** option won't get you to switch between all of them. All you have to do is to hold down the **Alt** button and then press the **Tab** continuously till it navigates to your desired window.

As you press the **Tab**. Don't release the **Alt** key.

Ctrl + Alt + Tab

This one is just like the option we just talked about. Except, you won't have to hold down the **Alt + key**. When you press this combo, all the windows will be opened to you just like the **Alt** key will do but this time it will remain like that.

This is the Tab Switch Freeze. Instead of letting you to just jump between windows and programs you just opened recently, you'll be able to see all the items that you've opened on your computer.

Then you can then switch to the one you would like to open. You can make use of the same **Tab** key or you just use the left and right controls to navigate through the windows

Windows key + R

This will have you opening up the **Run** dialog box

Windows key + A

When you get notifications they show up at the edge of your screen for a few seconds. You have those few seconds to select it and attend to the matter. If you wait any longer, it will disappear.

But you can still access the notification by going to the **Action Center**. Normally you have to go the corner of the display to access it. It is the icon that's just before the Date and Time. Yes, that one.

But the problem with that is it's too far. With **Windows key + A**, you'll get to it much faster. Just press it once and the Action Center opens up

Windows key + T

This is another method of switching through Windows. When you press the **Windows key + T**. you'll move through the options in the taskbar.

As you press **T** continuously, you'll see the taskbar run through the items on it. When it eventually gets to the app you want just hit **Enter** to open it up.

Alt + left or right

If you've opened many folders in File Explorer and you want to go back, this is a great option. Just hold the **Alt + left** and press left to go back.

You can press the **Alt + right** to return to the folder you just closed.

You should know that this shortcut will only get you to move through the folders that you've opened before. That is your search history. They will not get you to folders unless you have actually opened the folder before.

If you want to move a folder hierarchy. (That is the folder that houses the current folder you are in) you can just use **Alt + up**.

This shortcut does not just work for File Explorer only. The **Alt + right** and **Alt + left** shortcut can also work when you in a web browser. You'll be able to move forwards and backwards through the history of what you've searched for in the same tab.

No more looking for the back button on the screen, **Alt + left** does the trick. This works for most browsers like Chrome, Edge and Firefox.

Windows key + ,

It just gets better. If you would like to see the desktop and not minimize your apps this is the way to go

Pressing Windows key + , will get you to see the desktop briefly and return to your program. The longer you hold Windows key the longer the desktop stays.

Right-click taskbar + D

This is a good option to see what's going on in the computer if you opened different programs. All you have to do is just Right-click the taskbar at the bottom of screen and then press D

When you do this all the opened windows will be in cascade. That is will be stocked behind each other. When you use this cascade formation, you'll be able to find the apps that are open. If there's a program you don't want to use again, you can close it.

Right-click taskbar + U.

So you just tried the shortcut to cascade the windows. It worked, the windows are stacked behind each other now you want to get out of the mode.

You easily opt-out of the cascade option for the windows by Right-clicking on the taskbar then pressing U. this will revert the windows to the normal view and undo the cascade effect.

Before you actually do the 'uncascade' windows option, you should have used the cascade option first.

Right-click taskbar + E

The cascading option is great to see which programs are open on your computer. But there's a better way. It is the option to show windows stacked side-by-side. This does what it says. Its stacks the windows that are open.

All you have to do is Right-click the taskbar then press E. The way in which the windows will be stacked on your computer will depend on the number of apps or programs that you have opened and the type of documents and files that you have opened.

The windows will not be snapped to the corners, they'll just be resized and stacked. If you stacked the windows, and it has already served its purpose, you can always revert it back to the window you were in by Right-clicking the taskbar then pressing U.

Ctrl + F6

So let's say that you have two documents opened in Microsoft word. The normal way that you switch between them is by moving to the taskbar at the bottom, click the app icon then choose the document to enter.

Nice way. But too slow and it does reduce productivity. A quicker way; **Ctrl + F6**. This is the cycle program shortcut that will switch to the files that you opened for the same program.

If you opened, say 9 documents in Microsoft word, you can just press the **Ctrl + F6** and it will switch to the next document. Don't release the Ctrl and keep pressing F6. You'll see that it just keeps cycling through the files you opened.

Windows key + PrtSc

If you want to take screenshot on your computer, you can just press the PrtSc button on the keyboard. But that won't save it to the computer

Press **Windows key + PrtSc** and you'll be able to view the screenshot page in the pictures folder

Ctrl + M

Another option that you want to make use of to minimize all windows is the **Ctrl + M** shortcut. When you have many windows open, minimizing them one after the other with the minimize button at the top can be stressful

Especially when you have about 10 windows opened at once. **Ctrl + M** minimizes them all at once.

Ctrl + W

As you work with many files that are open in Windows 10, you may want to close out of a document but don't want to close out of the program itself. That was what this shortcut was made.

When you hit **Ctrl + W**, the current files that you make use of will be closed but the app will still be open.

What this means is if you hit **Ctrl + W** on a word document, the current files will be closed but Microsoft word itself will still be opened. You can then open another file. You will also be given to option to choose Save or Don't Save

You also make use of this **Ctrl + W** shortcut when you're in the multitasking view. You'll be able to use it to close any files that is opened at that moment.

Alt + F4

This shortcut should not be mistaken for **Ctrl + W**. The **Alt + F4** shortcut will not only quit the current file that you are working on but it will close you out of the application itself. When you press it, you'll also be given the option for Save or Don't Save.

When you press the **Alt + F4** on a word document, Windows will close any word document that is opened and also close Microsoft word. This very different from the **Ctrl + W** that only closes you out of the current file that is opened.

But that's not the only thing **Alt + F4** does. If you are on your windows desktop and you press the **Alt + F4** shortcut, you'll get the option to shut down your computer

If you are working on a file and you want to shutdown very quickly, you can just press **Ctrl + M**

to minimize all the windows that are open then
press **Alt + F4** to shut down your computer

Alt + Shift + D

This is a great way to insert the date very quickly. Pressing **Alt + Shift + D** will paste the date in format set is in your computer. **Alt + Shift + T** will get to paste the current time where the cursor is in a document.

Ctrl + N

When you're in Microsoft office suite, your go-to option for creating a new document should be the **Ctrl + N** shortcut. You can create new blank files very quickly and easily.

So if you working on Microsoft PowerPoint and you hit the **Ctrl + N**, a new presentation that you can work with will be opened to you.

Ctrl + N is also be very useful when you're managing your files with the Windows File Explorer. When you press the combo from File Explorer, you'll be given a new window that you can work with. Now you have 2 windows for the File Explorer. Snap it to split screen and you'll be able to drag and drop files into different folders.

If you created a window by opening Windows File Explorer afresh, you'll be shown the homepage.

But by using Ctrl + N, you'll be given a replica of the folder you're in but in a different window.

Ctrl + Shift + N

Still on File Explorer hacks. If you are in a folder and you want to create a new folder, you just have to hit **Ctrl + Shift + N** and a new blank folder will be created.

With this method you can easily create folders on the fly without stress. You'll be able to organize files quicker leading to better productivity.

Normally you will have to right click an empty space in the file explorer, chose New, then select folder. That method is long and stressful. It even makes one reconsider creating a new folder when one thinks of the process he has to go through.

But now, Ctrl + Shift + N makes it ever easier

Ctrl + Shift + >

This is a quick way to increase the size of a text. Instead of moving all the way up simply pressing **Ctrl + Shift + >** will do the trick

Ctrl + Shift + <

With **Ctrl + Shift + >**, you'll be able to decrease the size of the selected text. To decrease the size even further, keep pressing the > while the Ctrl + Shift is still held down

Right click + W + document

Creating a new folder with **Ctrl + Shift + N** is a fast and easy way to create empty folders. But what if you want to create new file without entering the program.

Yes it is possible to create a new document and not get into the application itself. You can do this for any Microsoft office application.

If you want to create a new blank document of an application, you just have to

1. Right click an area in the folder you want to the document to be
2. Press **W** to get to the New option
3. Choose the type of file you want to open

When you choose the file type, you'll see a new document of the application will be created. It will have the default name so you may have to enter a new one.

The file is created. And you did all this without having to open the application itself.

Windows key + +

Have you been finding yourself squinting to find out what is written on the screen of your computer? You may enlarged the text size for the application but maybe that's not enough or you don't want it zoomed in permanently.

Your next option is to use the **Windows key + +** shortcut. When you press the combo, you'll see the items on your screen become magnified. That's because you just opened the magnifier.

If you want to get a more zoomed in view you keep pressing the +. Just make sure that you don't release the Windows key.

Windows key + -

This does the same as the previous shortcut; magnifier. Except this one does the opposite; it zooms out. The zooming out does not happen when you're in the normal view of the screen.

There nothing to zoom out from at that point. But when you use the **Windows key + +** shortcut, you can easily use the **Windows key + +** shortcut to reverse the effect.

Ctrl + End

If you are using Microsoft word or any other word editing program, one easy way to go the end of the is to use Ctrl + End. The normal way to do it is by using the slider at the right side of the page.

Then you drag it to the end, but that's okay. But why would you use that when you've got **Ctrl + End**

Ctrl + Home

The opposite of the last option. You'll be able to use the **Ctrl + Home** shortcut to move directly to the beginning of the document.

Shift + Home

When you want to highlight a document in word, the normal procedure is to click and drag to the end of the word.

Not only is that method slow when it comes to highlighting all the texts in the same line, but you can select something else. The **Shift + Home** shortcut makes it easier

When you use the shortcut, the word from the cursor to the beginning of the line will be selected.

Shift + End.

This does the opposite of the previous shortcut. **Shift + End** will highlight from the end of the text to where the cursor is.

DISCLAIMER

In as much as the author believes beginners will find this book helpful in learning Windows 10 shortcuts, it is only a small reference guide. It should not be relied upon solely for all Windows 10 shortcuts, tricks and troubleshooting. s

ABOUT THE AUTHOR

Stephen Rock has been a certified apps developer and tech researcher for more than 12 years. Some of his 'how to' guides have appeared in a handful of international journals and tech blogs. He loves rabbits.

www.ingramcontent.com/pod-product-compliance
Lightning Source LLC
Chambersburg PA
CBHW031230050326
40689CB00009B/1550